Focus on Drugs
and the Brain

Focus on Drugs and the Brain

A Drug-Alert Book

David Friedman
Illustrated by David Neuhaus

TWENTY-FIRST CENTURY BOOKS
FREDERICK, MARYLAND

Published by
Twenty-First Century Books
38 South Market Street
Frederick, Maryland 21701

Printed in the United States of America

10 9 8 7 6 5 4 3 2 1

Library of Congress Cataloging in Publication Data

Friedman, David
Focus on Drugs and the Brain
Illustrated by David Neuhaus

(A Drug-Alert Book)
Includes bibliographical references
Summary: Describes the use and misuse
of drugs and their effects on the brain.
1. Drug abuse—Juvenile literature.
2. Brain—Effect of drugs on—Juvenile literature.
3. Psychoactive drugs—Physiological effect—Juvenile literature.
[1. Brain—Effect of drugs on. 2. Drugs. 3. Drug abuse.]
I. Neuhaus, David, ill. II. Title.
III. Series: The Drug-Alert Series.
RC564.3.F75   1990
615'.788—dc20   89-28417   CIP   AC
ISBN 0-941477-95-9

Table of Contents

Introduction

"Baby Saved by Miracle Drug!" "Drug Bust at Local School!" Headlines like these are often side by side in your newspaper, or you may hear them on the evening news. This is confusing. If drugs save lives, why are people arrested for having and selling them?

The word "drug" is part of the confusion. It is a word with many meanings. The drug that saves a baby's life is also called a medicine. The illegal drugs found at the local school have many names—names like pot, speed, and crack. But one name for all of these illegal drugs is dope.

Some medicines you can buy at your local drugstore or grocery store, and there are other medicines only a doctor can get for you. But whether you buy them yourself or need a doctor to order them for you, medicines are made to get you healthy when you are sick.

Dope is not for sale in any store. You can't get it from a doctor. Dope is bought from someone called a "dealer" or a "pusher" because using, buying, or selling dope is against the law. That doesn't stop some people from using dope. They say they do it to change the way they feel. Often, that means they are trying to run away from their problems. But when the dope wears off, the problems are still there—and they are often worse than before.

There are three drugs we see so often that we sometimes forget they really are drugs. These are alcohol, nicotine, and caffeine. Alcohol is in beer, wine, and liquor. Nicotine is found in cigarettes, cigars, pipe tobacco, and other tobacco products. Caffeine is in coffee, tea, soft drinks, and chocolate. These three drugs are legal. They are sold in stores. But that doesn't mean they are always safe to use. Alcohol and nicotine are such strong drugs that only adults are allowed to buy and use them. And most parents try to keep their children from having too much caffeine.

Marijuana, cocaine, alcohol, nicotine, caffeine, medicines: these are all drugs. All drugs are alike because they change the way our bodies and minds work. But different drugs cause different changes. Some help, and some harm. And when they aren't used properly, even helpful drugs can harm us.

Figuring all this out is not easy. That's why The Drug-Alert Books were written: so you will know why certain drugs are used, how they affect people, why they are dangerous, and what laws there are to control them.

Knowing about drugs is important. It is important to you and to all the people who care about you.

David Friedman, Ph.D.
Consulting Editor

Dr. David Friedman is Deputy Director of the Division of Preclinical Research at the National Institute on Drug Abuse.

Drugs, Drugs, Drugs

Drugs, drugs, drugs.

People everywhere are talking about drugs. In school and at home, you hear how harmful drugs are. Maybe you even know someone who has gotten in trouble with drugs.

Drugs, drugs, drugs.

It might seem that all you ever hear about is drugs.

If you pick up a newspaper or magazine, you are sure to see headlines about illegal drugs. When you listen to the radio or watch television, you are sure to hear stories about drug abuse. Every day, there are new reports about the spread of drugs, about drugs and crime, and especially about drugs and young people.

Why do drugs cause so many problems? Why do people use them? Why do they get people in so much trouble?

One reason is that many drugs change the way the brain works. They change the way people think, feel, and behave. The drugs that do this are called psychoactive drugs. The word "psyche" means "mind," and "active" comes from the word "act." A psychoactive drug is one that acts on the brain.

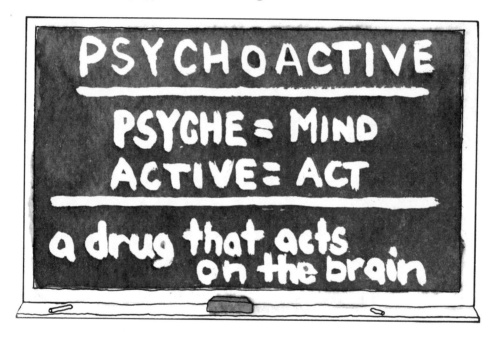

When people talk about drugs, they usually mean illegal drugs, like marijuana, cocaine, and PCP. We call these kinds of psychoactive drugs "dope." Most people know that dope is dangerous.

Not all psychoactive drugs are illegal. But even the legal psychoactive drugs are dangerous to use.

- Alcohol is a psychoactive drug. It is found in beer and wine. It is also found in liquor, like whiskey, gin, and rum. This psychoactive drug is so strong that it is legal only for adults.

- Nicotine is a psychoactive drug. It is found in tobacco products, like cigarettes, pipe tobacco, and chewing tobacco. This psychoactive drug is also very strong. Like alcohol, it is legal only for adults.

- Caffeine is also a psychoactive drug. It is found in coffee, tea, chocolate, and cola soft drinks. This psychoactive drug is not as strong as other drugs. It is legal for both adults and children. But it can be harmful if people use too much of it.

- Many medicines contain psychoactive drugs. Some medicines which contain psychoactive drugs, like cough syrup and cold remedies, can be bought by anyone. But if they are not used properly, they can be harmful, too. Other medicines are so strong that they can be ordered only by a doctor.

Drugs, drugs, drugs. Some are illegal; some are not. Some drugs are legal for adults but illegal for kids. Some drugs are legal for everybody but can still be harmful. Some drugs harm, and some drugs help. But even the helpful drugs can hurt us.

It's confusing, isn't it?

That's why this book was written: to help you make sense of drugs. It *is* confusing. After all, drugs are everywhere we turn. They're not just sold on street corners by "pushers" and "dealers." You can see them in grocery stores. There are even stores called "drug stores." You see people enjoying beer and wine on television. If alcohol is dangerous, why do they show so many people using it? You are told not to smoke, yet you know adults who do. Adults use drugs every day, yet they warn young people to "Just Say No" to drugs.

What is going on here?

It is very important for you to know what drugs are and what they do because you live and will grow up in a world where drugs are all around you. You live and will grow up in a world where you have to make decisions about drugs.

This book will help you make the right decisions. To do that, you need the facts. You need to know what a drug is and what different kinds of drugs do to the brain. You need to know how people get in trouble with drugs and what can be done to help them.

Drugs, drugs, drugs. You can't run and hide from drugs. But if you have the facts, you can make sense of drugs. You can make sense of all this talk about drugs. And you can make your own life a happy and healthy one.

Why People Use Drugs

People have always used psychoactive drugs. Our ancestors learned how to make alcohol before they learned how to make soap! Ancient writings show that psychoactive drugs have been used for thousands of years to try to cure diseases. Medicine men thought that certain drugs would drive out the evil spirits that made people sick. Psychoactive drugs were

also used as part of religious ceremonies. People would take drugs to try to "get in touch" with the gods. These drugs were also used on many other occasions, such as celebrating a new friendship or preparing to go to war.

But why do people use psychoactive drugs today?

When people use a drug that acts on the brain, it makes them feel different. That is why many people use psychoactive drugs. They use drugs because they *want* to feel different. They might want to feel more relaxed if they are worried or tense. They might want to feel happy if they are sad or depressed. They might want to feel more energetic if they are tired or bored.

There are many reasons why people start using drugs:

- Some people think taking drugs is fun and exciting. They take drugs to get a different feeling or just to try something new.

- Some people take drugs to run away from their problems. Their lives are filled with so much pain and unhappiness that they turn to drugs to try to change the way they feel.

- Some people take drugs because their friends do. They don't want to be left out of the crowd.

- Some people think taking drugs will make them "cool" or glamorous. They think taking drugs is a grown-up thing to do.

But these are not the only reasons why some people use psychoactive drugs.

Some people use psychoactive drugs as medicine. Doctors prescribe such drugs for a variety of reasons. Some psychoactive drugs help to control pain. In other cases, doctors want to change the mood or behavior of a patient. The right drug can help the patient lead a better life.

Some people use psychoactive drugs without even knowing it. They know that a cup of coffee or a candy bar gives them an extra lift, but they don't know why. They know that a mug of beer or a glass of wine helps them to relax, but they don't know why.

And some people take drugs because they are addicted to them. They feel sick without drugs. They find it hard to stop taking them even if they want to. They can't go a day without drugs.

Whatever the reason for doing it, changing the brain with a psychoactive drug is very serious. It can be very dangerous to change the way the brain works. The key to understanding why these drugs are so dangerous is the brain. If we want to know how drugs work, the first thing we need to know is how the brain works without drugs.

So let's explore the world of the brain.

The World of the Brain

Explorers may go to the farthest reaches of outer space or to the deepest parts of the ocean, but they will not find a more amazing, a more mysterious, or a more complex world than that of the human brain.

Do you know what the brain really is?

It is a mass of special cells called nerve cells, or neurons, and a giant tangle of nerve fibers that connect the neurons. The brain only weighs about three pounds. It is not much bigger than a pair of fists. If you could touch it, you could stick your finger right into it, like a bowl of custard. So it's a good idea that the brain sits inside the hard bones of your head. It needs a place like that to be safe from injury.

But the brain is much more than just a mass of cells. The brain is what makes us human beings. It is what makes each one of us a *different* human being. The brain is what gives each one of us a mind of our own. Without the brain, there wouldn't be any us.

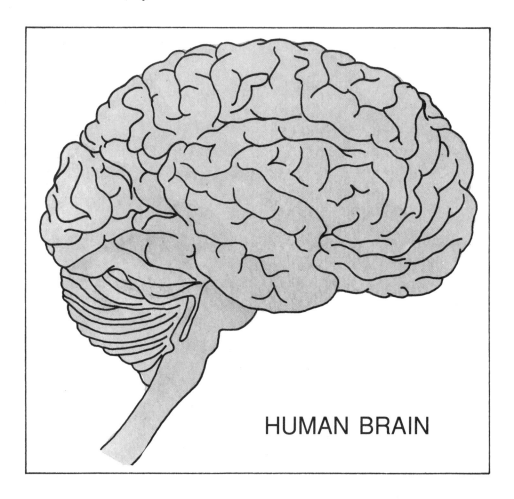

HUMAN BRAIN

The brain controls everything we do: things we hardly ever bother to think about, like breathing, and things we have to practice and practice, like playing the piano or catching a football. But whatever it is, the brain tells our bodies what to do and how to do it.

The brain controls everything we feel. Are you hungry? Your brain is saying you need food. Are you tired? Your brain is saying you need sleep. Feeling happy? Feeling sad? Hopeful or afraid? Your brain does your feeling for you.

Your brain also does your thinking for you. The brain is a wonderful thinking machine. It can solve problems, make plans, and imagine almost anything. It can also do something no machine can possibly do. It can make its own decisions. The brain gives us the ability to make choices about our lives. The ability to choose is what makes a human being different from a machine. The ability to choose is what makes human beings different from other animals.

Let's think about that for a minute. It's not as simple as you might think. We're able to make lots of different choices. But there are some things we are not able to do. For example, we cannot choose not to breathe. We can hold our breath if we want, but sooner or later the brain is going to make us breathe. We can try to stay awake when we are tired, but no matter how hard we try, sooner or later the brain will make us sleep.

It seems that we are able to do some things and not able to do others. How can that be?

The answer lies in the way the brain works. To understand how it works, you need to know how it is put together.

The human brain is like a building with two floors. The bottom floor controls our basic needs or drives. The top floor controls our thoughts and ideas.

Hungry? The hypothalamus, a part of the bottom floor of the brain, is saying you need food. Tired? The brain stem, another part of the bottom floor of the brain, is saying you need sleep. The bottom floor of the brain is in charge of the basic drives that keep us alive.

When we feel hunger, we try to find food to eat. When we feel tired, we try to find a place to lie down and sleep. It feels good to satisfy our basic needs. It gives us pleasure. Like other feelings, the feeling of pleasure comes from the brain.

There is an important area at the top of the brain stem that controls this feeling of pleasure. It is called the pleasure center. When this area of the brain gets turned on, we feel good. The things that help us survive—food and drink, rest and sleep—turn on the pleasure center.

The bottom floor of the brain is designed for survival. The parts of the brain on this floor tell us to get the things we need to survive. The hypothalamus and the brain stem drive us to satisfy these basic needs. When we do, we get a

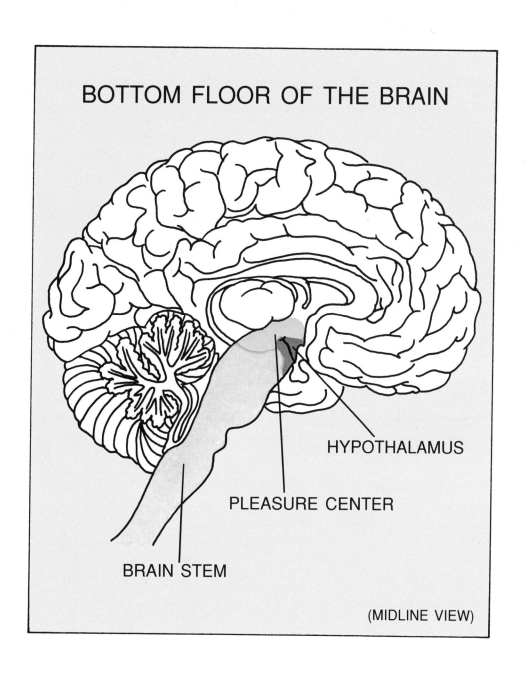

BOTTOM FLOOR OF THE BRAIN

HYPOTHALAMUS

PLEASURE CENTER

BRAIN STEM

(MIDLINE VIEW)

feeling of pleasure. The pleasure center helps us stay alive by making us feel good when we get the things that we need to survive. The drive for this feeling of pleasure helps to keep us alive.

The bottom floor of the brain looks alike in all animals. Some animals, like fish and reptiles, have brains with little more than a bottom floor. They eat and drink, they sleep and breathe, they reproduce their kind. With their bottom-floor brains, that is just about all they are able to do.

The brains of other animals—like rats, cats, monkeys, and humans—are more complicated. In addition to a bottom floor, they have a top floor in their brains. This top floor, called the cerebral cortex, is the thinking part of the brain.

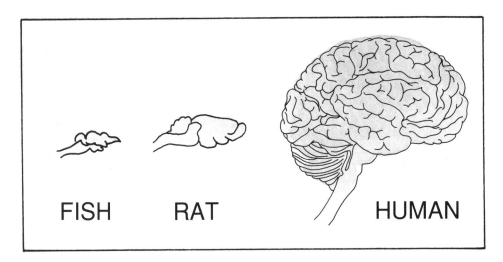

FISH   RAT   HUMAN

The cortex in humans is much bigger than it is in other animals. That is why humans are so smart and why they can do so many things other animals can't. That is why we can choose to do and think what we want.

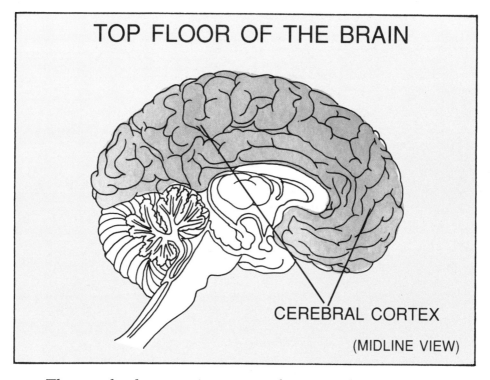

TOP FLOOR OF THE BRAIN

CEREBRAL CORTEX

(MIDLINE VIEW)

The cerebral cortex is constantly at work:

- getting and examining information

- making decisions and sending out commands

- learning new things and storing new information

The human cortex is made up of four different sections called lobes. These lobes are made up of many different parts, each with its own job to do. These parts are called cortical areas. Here is a picture of the different lobes of the cortex and what the cortical areas do:

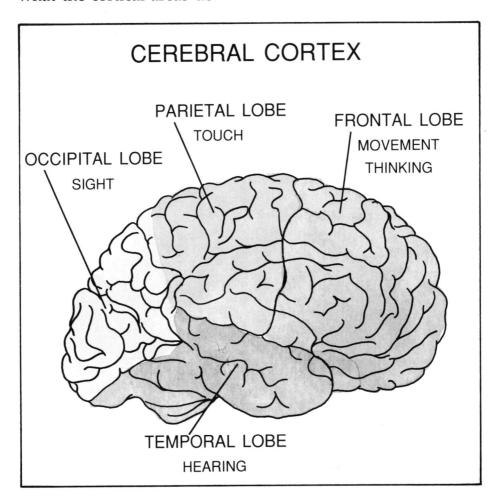

CEREBRAL CORTEX

PARIETAL LOBE
TOUCH

FRONTAL LOBE
MOVEMENT
THINKING

OCCIPITAL LOBE
SIGHT

TEMPORAL LOBE
HEARING

- The back end of the cortex is called the occipital lobe. Its job is to see for us. This part of the cortex receives messages from the nerve cells in our eyes so that we can see the world around us.

- Just in front of the occipital lobe is the parietal lobe. It receives messages from the nerve cells in our skin so that we can feel the world around us.

- The front half of the brain is the frontal lobe. Part of the frontal lobe is in charge of movement. It sends out messages to our muscles so that we can move. Another part of the frontal lobe is called the prefrontal cortex. Here is where we do a lot of our thinking: where we make decisions, plan for the future, and understand complex ideas.

- The lower part of the cortex is the temporal lobe. A part of this area, just below the touch and movement areas, is in charge of hearing. This part of the cortex receives messages from the nerve cells in the ears so that we can hear the world around us.

You could almost say that a human being has two brains in one. On the top floor, there is the brain that helps us to understand the world. On the bottom floor, there is the brain that helps us to take care of our basic needs and drives.

The Battle of the Brains

Sometimes, the two floors of the brain don't agree on what to do. It's like a battle of the brains.

Have you ever been so tired that you had to go to sleep even though you didn't really want to? You wanted to stay up; but one yawn followed another, your eyes got heavier and heavier, and before you knew it, you nodded off.

What happened? Why couldn't you keep yourself awake? The reason is that one part of your brain was stronger than the other. The brain stem was stronger than the cerebral cortex. Your need for sleep was stronger than your desire to stay awake. In the battle of the brains, your brain stem won out.

This is one example of how the brain helps us stay alive and healthy. It was more important for you to get some sleep than it was for you to stay awake. So it was a good thing that the bottom floor won the battle of the brains. And it felt good to go to sleep. Satisfying your need for sleep turned on the pleasure center. Not only did you get what you needed, but it gave you pleasure to get it.

Many different things turn on the brain's pleasure center: a cool drink of water on a hot day, a big meal when you are hungry, a warm house on a winter night, a soft bed when you are tired. These are normal and natural pleasures. These are the things that help you survive and lead a healthy life.

But other things turn on the pleasure center, too. Many psychoactive drugs—drugs like alcohol and cocaine, heroin and nicotine—also turn on the pleasure center. That's why people feel different when they use these drugs. The problem is that drugs are not a normal or natural way to turn on the pleasure center. They turn on the pleasure center too easily and too much. In fact, the brain gets more pleasure from some drugs than it does from food, drink, rest, and sleep.

Psychoactive drugs can turn the brain against itself. The brain of a drug user begins to want the feeling it gets from drugs more than it wants the pleasure it gets from the very things we need to survive. The brain of a drug user begins to think that drugs are as important as the things we need to survive. It wants alcohol, not food. It wants cocaine, not sleep. It wants a dangerous and destructive drug, not a healthy and nourishing pleasure.

The brain of a drug user is no longer working in a natural and normal way. It is turned on by drugs.

But how are drugs able to turn on a part of the brain? How are they able to make the brain need them? To understand this, you need to know more about how the brain works. You need to understand the human message center.

The Human Message Center

The brain is a busy place. It's working 24 hours a day, sending and receiving messages. These messages travel along the networks of nerve cells known as the nervous system.

Let's see how this works.

Suppose you read a word that is new to you. You don't know what it means. What do you do? Of course you turn to the dictionary and find out what it means. Now, you are able to make sense out of what you're reading. Simple, right?

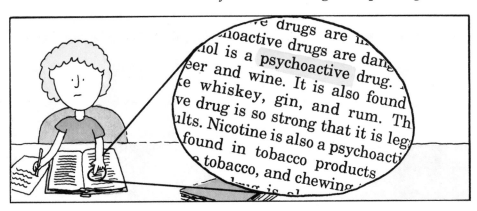

Well, it's really not so simple.

First, you have to see the word. That's one job of the brain. The brain sees the world around us.

"The brain sees?" you might ask. "You must mean the eyes see."

There are millions of nerve cells in the eyes, but the eyes don't really see anything. What they do is send information about the outside world to the brain. It is only when the brain receives this information from the nerve cells in the eyes that we are able to see things.

But what does the brain do with all this information?

- The brain examines this information. It compares the new information with the other information it already has.

- The brain decides whether the new information is important or not. Then, it decides whether to keep this information.

- The brain stores this information if it is important. It keeps the new information in its memory.

- The brain thinks about this information. It uses the new information to help us react to the outside world.

Now, what about that new word? Your eyes send information about the new word to your brain. The brain checks your memory to see if the word is already there. But this word is not in your memory.

What next? The brain tries to figure out the meaning of this word by comparing it with other words you already know. Your brain is talking to itself to see if it can come up with some idea about this new word. Your brain is thinking.

Sometimes, no matter how hard you think, you just can't come up with an answer. Your brain doesn't have enough information to work with. You're stumped.

But not for long. Your brain starts thinking about ways to get the information it needs. It sends a message to the eyes to read the word again. Then, it instructs you to do something else: "Check the dictionary," it says.

The brain sends a message to your arm, telling it to pick up the dictionary. It sends a message to your hands telling them to turn to the right page. And it sends a message to your eyes telling them to read the meaning of this new word.

Your eyes send this new information to your brain. Your brain now has the information it needs to understand the meaning of this new word. And it stores the word and its meaning in its memory files. The next time you read this word, your brain will know what it means.

The brain constantly receives messages from the nerve cells in your eyes. Your ears, nose, mouth, and skin work in the same way. They send messages to your brain about what you hear, smell, taste, and feel. These messages tell the brain what is happening in the world around you.

The brain sends and receives billions of messages every day. Billions and billions! How does the brain do it?

The brain sends and receives messages along a network of nerve cells, or neurons. Neurons have a very special job to do. Each one is designed to receive information, examine information, and send information to other neurons.

- To receive information, each neuron has special branches called dendrites. On the branches of each dendrite, there are special places called receptors to receive messages.

- To examine information, each neuron has a cell body. The cell body decides what to do with the information it receives. If it decides the information is important, the cell body will send it to another neuron.

- To send information, each neuron has a long cable called an axon. It looks and acts like a telephone wire. The axon receives the message from the cell body and sends it to the receptors on the dendrites of another neuron.

From neuron to neuron, messages are passed along the nervous system. Between each neuron and the next one, there is a gap called a synapse. It takes special chemicals to get a message across these gaps.

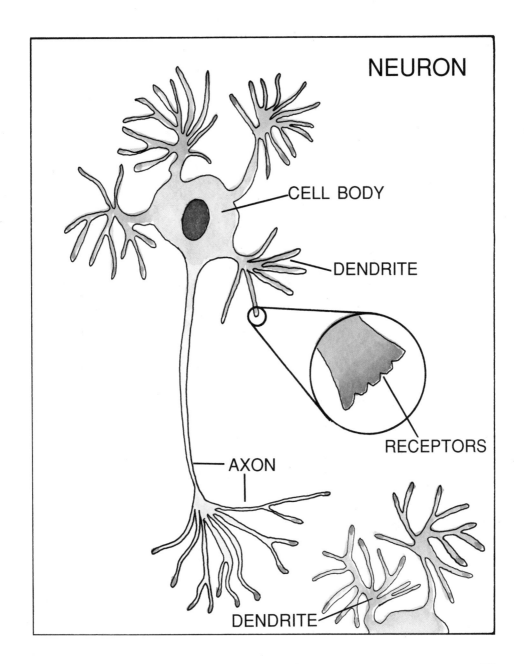

NEURON

CELL BODY

DENDRITE

RECEPTORS

AXON

DENDRITE

These chemicals, called transmitters, take messages from the axon of one nerve cell and send it to the receptors of another nerve cell.

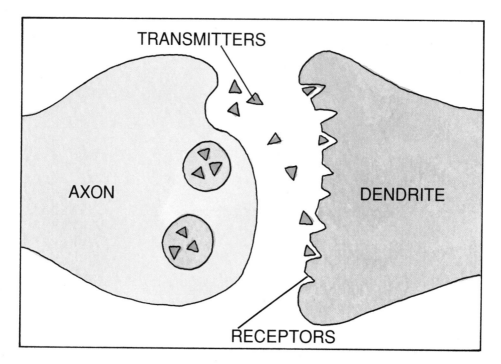

A transmitter is like a key. A receptor is like a lock. When the key fits the lock, a nerve cell is turned on and does its job. When the key does not fit the lock, a nerve cell is not turned on and won't send or receive a message. The whole nervous system depends on these locks and keys. When they work properly, messages speed along the network of nerves to and from the brain.

But when psychoactive drugs are used, these locks and keys don't work properly. Drugs disrupt the way messages are sent to and from the brain.

Some drugs slow down the number of messages or even shut down message routes that should be open. Important messages are unable to get through. Other drugs speed up the number of messages too fast. There are so many messages getting through that the brain can't make sense of them. Still other drugs interfere with the work of the brain in ways that we do not fully understand. Whether they speed up or slow down the brain, psychoactive drugs change the way the brain normally works.

That can be a good thing. Some drugs are used to stop pain because they block the pain messages going to the brain. Doctors can use psychoactive drugs to change the brain in ways that are helpful to us.

But changing the brain with psychoactive drugs can be a very harmful thing, too. Using drugs can change the locks and keys of the brain's pleasure center. When that happens, it seems that only drugs have the right keys to unlock the pleasure center. So people need drugs to feel normal. They need drugs the same way we need food or sleep. They are on the road to drug addiction.

What Drugs Do to the Brain

In order for them to work, psychoactive drugs have to get to the brain. They are carried to the brain in the body's bloodstream. But how do they get into the bloodstream? There are several different ways. Here are some of them:

- Some drugs can be swallowed. They pass from the stomach and intestines into the bloodstream. That's what happens when someone takes a spoonful of cough syrup or drinks a beer.

- Some drugs can be injected. The drug is put directly into the body by a hypodermic needle. That's what happens when drug users give themselves shots of heroin.

- Some drugs can be inhaled. The lungs breathe in the drug and send it on to the bloodstream. That's what happens when someone smokes a cigarette.

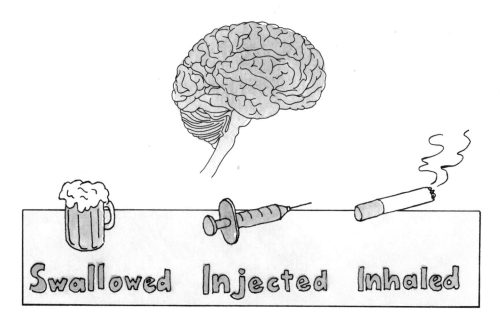

No matter how they get to the brain, psychoactive drugs are dangerous. They are especially harmful for young people. Some drugs may help you when you are sick, but you should only use them when a doctor or parent tells you to. And you should take them exactly as you are told. Even a helpful drug can hurt you if it is not taken properly.

Psychoactive drugs change the way the brain works. But not all psychoactive drugs change the brain in the same way. Different drugs do different things to the message system of the brain. Some calm us down and make us feel sleepy. Others make us feel active and energetic. Still others make the world look strange and unusual to us.

• Depressants

Drugs that slow the brain down are called depressants. Alcohol is a depressant. So are sleeping pills. You may have heard of tranquilizers, sedatives, or barbiturates. These are all depressants. They are often called "downers."

Depressants first slow down the top floor of the brain, the cerebral cortex. A small amount of a depressant makes some people feel calm and relaxed. But a larger amount of a depressant will disrupt the messages of the brain that control movement, speech, and thought. That's why people who are drunk, for example, can't move or speak well. That's why they can't think clearly or remember things. And too much of a depressant will turn off the brain entirely. The brain may stop sending out the messages that tell our lungs to breathe—and that means death.

• Opiates

Opiates are a group of drugs made from the poppy, a flower with a milky white juice called opium. Codeine is an opiate. So are morphine and heroin. These drugs are also called narcotics.

Opiates are sometimes used as medicines. They are found in pain relievers. These drugs block the pain messages going to the brain. Opiates are also found in cough medicines. They block the signals that tell us to cough. Opiates are sometimes used to control diarrhea.

But opiates can also turn on the brain's pleasure center. People who use heroin, for example, say they feel an intense "rush" of pleasure. It lasts for only a short time, but the pleasure center is so turned on by the drug that it is hard for people to resist using it again and again.

• Steroids

Steroids are used by some athletes to become bigger and stronger. Steroids help them to build up muscles, to train and exercise harder, and to recover from injuries more quickly.

Steroids are especially dangerous to young people. They interfere with the way the body normally grows. Steroids can cause acne and baldness. They can damage the kidneys and heart. They may make it impossible for young men to have children later in life.

Steroids also change the way the brain works. Some people say that using steroids regularly makes them feel self-confident. They feel powerful and more manly. But steroids are known to make people moody, irritable, and easily upset. Steroid users may have violent temper tantrums, sometimes called "roid rages." And like other drugs, it is hard to stop using steroids. Some people who stop using steroids get very depressed. Some even think about killing themselves.

• Hallucinogens

Drugs that change the way the world looks to us are called hallucinogens. LSD and PCP are hallucinogens. They are also known as "psychedelic" drugs. Marijuana is a drug with similar effects.

Hallucinogens change the way the world looks to the people who use them. They make the everyday world look like a strange and different place. To many people, they make the world seem confusing and frightening. People who use LSD, also known as "acid," may become scared of the world and think they are in great danger. People who use PCP, also known as "Angel Dust," may become angry and violent.

Like hallucinogens, marijuana, also known as "pot," changes the way people see the world. Like depressants, marijuana makes it hard for people to think clearly. Smoking pot can cause cancer and lung diseases. It hurts the body's immune system, making it easier for people to get sick.

• Stimulants

Drugs that speed up the way the brain works are called stimulants. Cocaine is a stimulant. So are amphetamines, also called "speed" or "uppers."

Stimulants speed up the brain in a dangerous way. People who use them become tense and irritable. They don't eat or sleep. Stimulants also make the heart work so fast that it can be damaged. Cocaine and amphetamines can even stop the messages from the brain that control the heart and lungs—the messages that keep us alive.

Caffeine is also a mild stimulant. It makes people feel more alert and energetic, but too much caffeine makes people easily upset and irritable. Too much caffeine has also been linked to heart disease, cancer, and birth defects.

• Nicotine

Nicotine is a drug found in tobacco products: cigarettes, cigars, chewing tobacco, pipe tobacco, and snuff.

Like stimulants, it speeds up the way the brain works. Nicotine makes some people feel more alert and energetic. Some people say it helps them to relax.

The most popular way to use nicotine is to smoke tobacco products. But tobacco smoke contains harmful chemicals and gases that cause heart and lung diseases. These chemicals and gases cause cancer of the lungs, mouth, and throat. Nicotine is a very addictive drug. That is why it is hard for people to stop using tobacco products even when they really want to.

The Road to Addiction

Psychoactive drugs change the way the brain works. The longer a person uses these drugs, the more the brain changes. In time, the brain changes so much that it thinks it needs drugs to stay alive.

Nobody wants to get hooked on drugs. That's not why people use drugs. Most people who use drugs, at first, believe they can handle drug use: "It won't happen to me," they say. "I'm not an addict." But using drugs is like standing on a slippery slope. It's easy to start sliding down. And once you start to slide, it's hard to stop.

We don't know *who* will become addicted to drugs. But we do know *how* people get addicted to drugs. We know the steps on the road to addiction. That is important knowledge for you to have. It may help you spot a drug problem before it gets out of hand. It may help prevent a drug problem from ever getting started.

• First use

Everyone who goes down the road to addiction begins by using drugs once. It may be nicotine: a cigarette on the way home from school. It may be alcohol: a drink of beer with friends on the weekend. It may be marijuana: a joint at a dance or party.

Nicotine, alcohol, and marijuana: these are sometimes called "gateway" drugs because they open the gate to drug problems. Some people think these drugs lead young people to use other illegal drugs. That might happen, but even if it doesn't, it is important to remember that nicotine, alcohol, and marijuana *are* dangerous drugs. It is important to remember that people can get hooked on them, too.

People don't need these drugs, and their bodies let them know it. Alcohol tastes terrible, and it makes people dizzy. Cigarette smoke and marijuana smoke burn the throat. So why don't people listen to their bodies and stop using drugs?

Many people do just that. They say "No" to drugs. In fact, most young people don't use drugs. We hear so much about drugs now that we might forget the simple fact that millions and millions of young people every day decide *not* to use drugs.

• Occasional use

Do you go along with the crowd? Lots of young people do. They may know people who smoke marijuana or drink beer. They may try these drugs, too.

Saying "No" to drugs is not always an easy decision to make. If your friends are using drugs, it can be difficult to say "No." The pressure to do what other people your own age are doing is called peer pressure.

There are many choices for young people to make. What music do you listen to? What clothes do you wear? How do you style your hair? It's only natural to want to do what your friends are doing. But there are also times when you have to think for yourself. There are times when you have to make tough decisions.

Young people who use drugs often do so because they give in to the pressure to fit in. They may think using drugs is a part of having fun. They may start to use drugs again and again—drinking beer at parties or smoking pot with their friends. They are learning the habit of drug use.

Deciding to use drugs is a choice some people make. They use drugs because they have made a decision to use them. They use drugs because they want to use them. Deciding not to use drugs is a choice people make, too. People who are just learning the habit of drug use can still make the decision to stop. They still have the ability to say "No" to drugs.

• Routine use

As time goes on, people who are learning the drug habit begin to use drugs more and more—and not just at parties or with friends. They like the way drugs make them feel—and they don't like the way they feel without drugs. They may start to use them every day.

People who use drugs are often trying to run away from problems. Having a fight with parents or friends, getting a bad report card, being cut from the team: there are hundreds of problems young people have to face as they grow up. (And problems don't go away when you're grown up, either. Then, there are grown-up problems!) Young people get lonely, they get scared, they get bored. (Adults do, too.)

It's not always easy to work out our problems. So some people, young people and adults, choose what seems to be an easy way out: they turn to drugs.

But drugs don't work to solve problems. They may help people forget a hard time, but that's just for a little while. Running away from problems doesn't make them go away. And young people who use drugs to run away from problems do not learn how to solve problems without drugs. They may grow up physically, but they don't grow up emotionally. They just keep running away.

Using drugs to run away from our problems only makes them worse. It causes trouble at school and at home. It makes people sick. Using illegal drugs turns people—even young people—into criminals. Using drugs makes a complete mess out of life.

Even worse, using drugs causes important changes in the way the brain works. It causes tolerance and dependence.

Tolerance is when people need more and more of a drug to change the way they feel. The amount of a drug that used to make them feel different no longer works. It's not that the drug is getting weaker. It's that the nerve cells of the brain get used to the drug. The drug no longer speeds up or slows down the work of the brain as much as it used to. So people need bigger and bigger doses of the drugs they use.

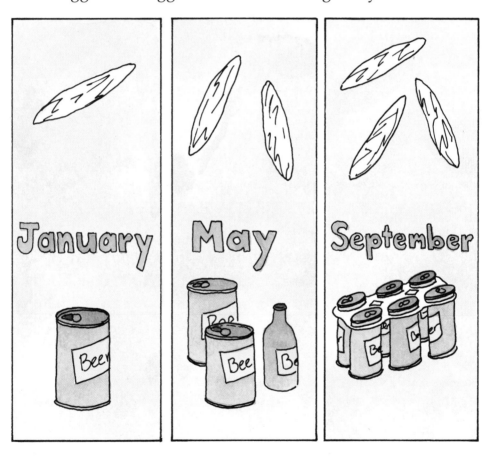

Drug use changes the way the brain works in another way. The brain of a drug user, in time, changes so that it *needs* the drugs to work properly, just as your body needs food or sleep. This need for drugs is called dependence.

Dependence on drugs means needing them more often. Needing drugs more often means different things for different people. It might mean needing a cigarette every 20 minutes. It might mean needing a shot of heroin every four hours. It might mean needing alcohol all of the time.

Dependence means that drug users need the drug in their bodies to feel normal. When the drug is taken away, drug users feel sick. This sick feeling is called withdrawal. The more people use drugs, the more dependent they become on them. The more dependent people become on drugs, the sicker they will feel without them. Withdrawal can often be so severe that people need medical treatment.

Dependence can also mean that drugs may have become the most important thing in a person's life. It can mean drug addiction.

• Addiction

What does it mean to be addicted to drugs? It means that the use of drugs has changed the brain so much that people feel they *must* have drugs. Their brains are telling them that they have no choice. They *must* find drugs. They *must* use drugs. The focus of their lives is drugs.

Being addicted means that *only* drugs will turn on the pleasure center. So addicts get little pleasure from life except when they are on drugs. Drugs have turned the brain against itself. Now, the brain thinks it needs drugs to stay alive and healthy. People who are addicted to drugs feel they need them the way other people feel they need food and sleep. Drug addicts no longer care about school or work. They no longer care about their families or friends. They don't even care about themselves. The only thing they care about is getting drugs, using drugs, and then getting more drugs.

Do you remember what was said about the brain in Chapter 3: how it is like an amazing thinking machine; how it can solve problems; and how it can decide things for itself? We said that the brain gives us the ability to make choices about our lives. People who are addicted to drugs no longer have the ability to choose whether or not to use drugs. They are driven by their own brains to use drugs.

Some people do not understand why drug addicts just don't kick the habit. They may ask, "Why don't addicts simply choose to stop?" They may think addicts don't want to stop using drugs because they are weak or bad. But addicts can't stop using drugs when they want to. Their drug addiction has become a sickness, and they will need help if they want to recover.

The Road to Recovery

We know the steps on the road to drug addiction. We know how drugs get people hooked. We also know the steps on the road to recovery from drug addiction. We know how people can get free of drugs and live drug-free lives.

The first step in the recovery from drug addiction is to admit that there is a problem. Drug addicts are experts at fooling themselves. An addict will deny that there is a drug problem even when it is obvious to everyone else.

Something has to make drug addicts see the truth. They may take too many drugs and get very sick, or they may get arrested for using or selling drugs. They may end up in the hospital; they may end up in jail. They may lose their jobs; they may lose their families. They may just get tired of their drug-dependent lives.

The second step in recovering from addiction is getting drugs out of the body. This is called "detoxification." A toxin is a poison, and detoxification means cleaning out the poison of drugs in the body. It usually means that an addict has to go through withdrawal sickness. That can be a difficult step, and it may need a doctor's attention. But the body and brain must be drug-free to work properly.

The third step in recovery is learning drug-free habits. Addicts have to learn how to be happy without drugs. Addicts have to learn how to face problems without drugs.

Many times there are other problems in an addict's life, problems that may have led to drug use in the first place. Addicts need the help of doctors and professional counselors both to understand these problems and to work to solve them without drugs. In drug treatment programs, addicts often get help from support groups. These groups are made up of other recovering addicts. In these groups, addicts talk to one another about their problems and try to help each other on the road to recovery.

Recovery from addiction may be the hardest thing a drug addict will ever have to do. It is not something most drug addicts can do on their own. But it is something they *can* do with the right kind of help.

There are many different kinds of treatment programs for drug addicts. Sooner or later, however, drug users will have to leave treatment and face the real world. It can be hard to get drugs out of the body. But for drug addicts, it is even harder to go back to the real world and live without drugs. They will probably go back to their old lives and their old friends. They will probably be offered drugs again. They will probably feel the urge to use drugs again.

The fourth step is the longest and hardest one of all. It is a step that addicts must take for the rest of their lives. That step is saying "No" to drugs, now and in the future. There is no cure for drug addiction. Drugs have changed the brains of addicts so much that it will never be safe for them to use drugs again. The only way to stop a drug habit is to stop using drugs once and for all.

Saying "No" to Drugs

You don't have to be an addict to be hurt by drugs. Drug use hurts everybody. It hurts people whether they use drugs or not.

You will grow up in a world where psychoactive drugs are everywhere. Some of these drugs will be illegal, and some will not. Some of these drugs will be medicines that can help you lead a better life. But all of these drugs, even medicines, will be able to hurt you.

You will grow up in a world that is confused about drugs. Some drugs are in the news every day, but others you may hear very little about. You will learn that some drugs, like marijuana and cocaine, are dangerous, yet you will often see adults using other drugs, like alcohol and nicotine. But all of these drugs, legal or not, can hurt you.

How can you make sense of this? One way is to know as much about drugs as you can: to know what they are and how they work. In this book, we have looked at psychoactive drugs and the brain. We have seen that psychoactive drugs change the brain. We have seen that these drugs can turn the brain against itself. We have seen that these drugs can trap people in dangerous drug habits.

We also saw that the brain gives people the ability to choose what kind of decisions they will make. It gives people the ability to choose what kind of life they will lead. You have the ability now to say "No" to drugs that will hurt you. You have the ability now to say "Yes" to a happy, healthy, and drug-free future.

Our ability to choose is a wonderful thing. But it can be lost. Drugs can take it away from us. This doesn't have to happen. And it won't if you know about drugs and have the courage and good sense to say "No" to them.

Glossary

addiction　the constant need or craving that makes people use drugs they know are harmful

axon　a long, wire-like cable extending from the cell body of a neuron; it sends messages to other neurons

brain stem　a part of the brain that is in charge of basic functions, such as heart rate and breathing

cell body　the central part of a neuron; it examines information received from other neurons

cerebral cortex　the part of the brain that is in charge of our thoughts and ideas

dendrite　a branch-like extension from the cell body of a neuron; it receives messages from other neurons

dependence　the way the body and brain need a drug to avoid feeling sick

detoxification　the process by which poisons are cleaned out of the body

hypothalamus　a part of the brain that is in charge of basic needs and drives, such as the need for food

lobe	one of four parts of the cerebral cortex; each lobe is in charge of specific functions of the brain
nervous system	the body system designed to carry information; it consists of the brain, spinal cord, and nerves
pleasure center	the part of the brain that is in charge of our feelings of pleasure
psychoactive drug	a substance that acts on the brain to change thoughts, feelings, and behavior
receptor	a special part of the dendrite that enables messages to be received
recovery	the process by which addicts learn to live without drugs
stimulant	a kind of drug that speeds up the work of the brain
synapse	the gap between neurons through which messages are passed from one cell to another
transmitter	a chemical used by the nervous system to carry messages from one neuron to another
tolerance	the way the body and brain need more and more of a drug to get the same effect
withdrawal	the sick feeling drug users get when they can't get the drugs they are dependent on

Index